BE

AND

DOCUMENTING THE ARCHITECTURE OF DISASTER

EYAL AND INES WEIZMAN

CONTENTS

History is increasingly presented as a series of catastrophes. The most common mode of this presentation is the before-and-after image – a juxtaposition of two photographs of the same place, at different times, before and after an event has taken its toll. Buildings seen intact in a 'before' photograph have been destroyed in the one 'after'. Neighbourhoods bustling with activity in one image are in ruins or under a layer of foul water in the next. Deforestations, contaminations, melting icebergs and drying rivers are represented in paired images that purport to show the consequences of rogue development, resource exploitation, war or climate change. It seems that almost any photograph taken today has the potential to become a 'before' to a devastating 'after' yet to come.

p. 53

The juxtaposition inherent in before-and-after photographs communicates not a slow process of transformation over time but, rather, a sudden or radical change. Forensic accounts, which seek to reconstruct what took place between the two moments in time, can sometimes involve intricate processes of interpretation that cross-reference before-and-after images with other forms of evidence. But more commonly before-and-after photographs are used to privilege a direct line of causality between a singular action and a unique effect. In before-and-after photographs, the event – whether natural, man-made or an entanglement of them both – is missing. Instead, it is captured in the transformation of space, thus calling for an architectural analysis. This spatial interpretation is called upon to fill the gap between the two images with a narrative, but that job is never straightforward.

The history of before-and-after images is as old as the history of photography. Indeed, they emerged from the limitations of the early photographic process. The few dozen seconds required for the exposure of a mid-19th-century photograph was too long a duration to record moving figures and abrupt events. The result was that most often people were missing from the image; only buildings and other elements of the urban fabric were registered. To capture an event, two photographs were necessary. The technique was thus useful in representing the consequences of urban conflicts, revolutionary action and large-scale urban reconstructions. Because the event was registered only through changes in the environment, those studying the result of violence needed to shift their attention from the figure (the individual or action) to the ground (the urban fabric or landscape).

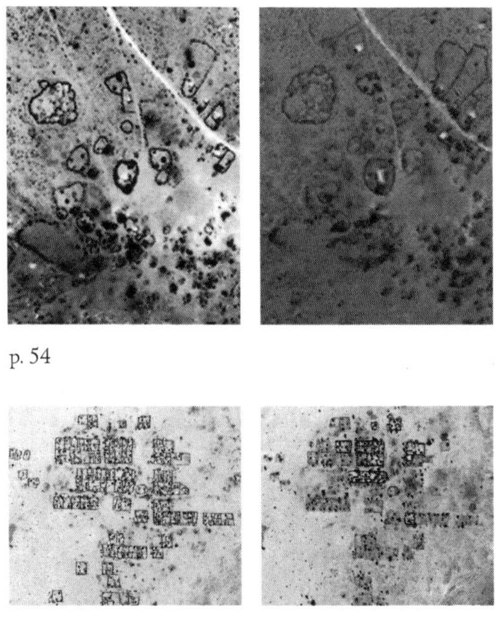

p. 54

p. 54

Today, the most common before-and-after images are satellite photographs, and they are once again the product of a limitation in the photographic process. The orbit times of satellites circumnavigating the planet means that they can only capture the same place at regular intervals. Because there is a time lag between each image (the fastest satellites can orbit the Earth every 90 minutes but at higher altitudes they take several hours), the crucial event is often missed. In addition, international regulations currently limit the resolution of publicly available satellite imagery to 50 cm per pixel (every 50 cm area is represented as a single, colour-coded surface). Higher-resolution images are available to state agencies, but the regulation limiting publicly available resolution was set so that they would not register the human body.[1]

Although this regulation was set because of concerns about privacy, it also has a security rationale. Not only are strategic sites camouflaged by the 50 cm pixel resolution, but the consequences of state violence and violations become harder to investigate. In Israel and the occupied territories an even more severe limitation on the resolution of satellite imagery requires that providers degrade their image to a resolution of 1 m per pixel.[2] This has the effect, intended no doubt, of limiting the ability of independent organisations to monitor state action within that area. Whether politically or technically motivated, the fact is that the limitation on resolution means that, 150 years after the invention of photography, the original problem persists: people are still not registered in the kind of before-and-after photographs that most commonly document destructive events.

The contemporary prevalence of before-and-after images shapes our perception of the world. It certainly opens up a new dimension in shifting our attention from the representation of the human agent to representations of territories and architecture, which also turns spatial analysis into an essential political tool. However, the crucial thing in before-and-after images is the gap between them, and these gaps can resist easy interpretation.

In order to unpack the politics of before-and-after images, it is vital to understand their history.

THE HISTORY OF THE BEFORE-AND-AFTER IMAGE

p. 55

Perhaps the earliest before-and-after photographs of an urban scene are a pair of daguerreotypes of the barricade in Paris's Rue Saint-Maur Popincourt. These were captured by Eugène Thibault from a hidden window, before and after a clash between workers and the National Guard led by General Lamoricière on Sunday, 25 June, 1848. Photography historian Marie Warner Marien has described the scene unfolding in this pair.[3] The 'before' image shows a sequence of two or three barricades that appear to have been assembled out of sand bags and cobblestones. Although the workers' neighbourhoods of the time were undergoing an unprecedented population explosion, we can see no one in the street and no one manning the barricade. Are they hiding or are they moving too fast to be captured by the camera? The 'after' image is blurry. The National Guard seems to have broken through. Artillery and other military equipment have been positioned at the place previously held by the defenders. The workers were defeated, killed in battle, captured or executed, but the violence and confusion of the battle are missing.

Not only is the action within this pair of before-and-after photographs subject to interpretation, but the meaning of the pairing itself has also changed with time. When printed in August 1848, in the reactionary (and, later, collaborationist) Parisian weekly *L'Illustration*, it was meant to convey the state's warning to the workers: this will be your fate if you rebel! But we can now see it as a testimony to the revolutionaries' resistance as they started to transform our world.

Even the presentation of this most minimal of sequences – a sequence of only two images – calls to mind other cultural forms and human experiences. First, it made imaginable the possibility of moving images, a decade before the movie was invented. In this context it could also be understood as a kind of very early montage: a form of construction in which images are commented upon, not by words, but by other images. Second, in this, as in all before-and-after photographs, the absence of the event from representation might be seen as analogous to the effects of trauma on memory. Psychological trauma erases or represses precisely those events that were hardest for the subject to experience, and these gaps forever keep any recollection incomplete and indeterminate. Contemporary legal theory now treats these memory lacunae as evidence in their own right – the very act of erasure is evidence of the trauma suffered by the subject. Similarly the gap between before-and-after images might also be considered as a reservoir of imagined images and possible histories.

Before-and-after photographs can also depict acts of destruction in a highly ambiguous way. For instance, the photographic sequence that began with Thibault and the breaking of the barricades was continued two decades later. The narrow streets and alleyways of the neighbourhoods that the workers of 1848 were trying to defend were largely destroyed in the 1860s and 1870s, as Georges-Eugène Haussmann carried out his rebuilding of Paris. This too would be captured by before-and-after photographs: for 16 years, beginning in 1862, Charles Marville, the official photographer of Paris, positioned his camera along the paths that Haussmann's avenues and vistas would cut before, during and after their destruction and reconstruction. Marville's images of the transformation of Paris were long misunderstood to be simply a nostalgic representation, a lament for the destruction of 'old Paris'. This assumption has been proven wrong by art historian Maria Morris Hambourg. Undertaking a forensic-like investigation, Hambourg located the points from which these photographs were taken. She plotted their locations on maps of both the old and the new Paris, demonstrating that Marville used Haussmann's plans to decide where to place his camera and how to compose his images.[4] She writes: '... just as Haussmann pencilled his straight boulevards across the Byzantine topography of Old Paris, so Marville worked along the path of the projected streets, photographing whatever would be levelled to make way for them .... Marville's pictures cut through the urban fabric almost as ruthlessly as Haussmann's pick-axe teams.'[5] Marville's work was complementary to Haussmann's plans. Indeed, his deliberately bleak views of uneven, curved streets with cobblestones and dilapidated houses would not have aroused feelings of nostalgia in the 19th century. The images he created describe a pre-modern urban scene – condemned precisely because it was blocking the path to modernisation – in order to juxtapose it with the idea of the modern, convenient, efficient and hygienic city of the future, all constructed *ex-nihilo* in the gap between the two pictures. The 'gaze' that Marville captured in his photographs turned the present into the future long before anything was actually destroyed and rebuilt.

Sometimes the question in before-and-after images is which is which. In her celebrated book, *Regarding the Pain of Others*, Susan Sontag discussed a photograph titled *The Valley of the Shadow of Death*, taken by English photographer Roger Fenton in 1855 during the Crimean war. In the photograph, which she claims is the first photograph of war, a roadway in a valley leading to Sebastopol is thickly scattered with cannonballs.

p. 56–57

Referring to another photograph by Fenton of the same site from the very same perspective but without the cannonballs on the road, she explained that 'many of the canonical images of early war photography turn out to have been staged, or to have had their subjects tampered with. After reaching the much-shelled valley approaching Sebastopol in his horse-drawn darkroom, Fenton made two exposures from the same tripod position: in the first version of the celebrated photo... the cannonballs are thick on the ground to the left of the road, but before taking the second picture – the one that is always reproduced – he oversaw the scattering of the cannonballs on the road itself.'[6]

In 'Crimean War Essay', the first chapter in his polemical book *Believing is Seeing*, Errol Morris sets out to prove Sontag wrong, or at least to challenge the ease of her assumption that the photograph with cannonballs on the road was taken *after* the one in which the cannonballs are to the side of the road. If Sontag's assumed order is wrong and the photograph with the cannonballs on the road was the first image, Morris claims, Fenton might have just cleared the road to allow his carriage to drive through.

To establish the temporal order in this pair of before-and-after photographs Morris travelled to the Crimea, where he searched for and found the exact perspective of Fenton's shot. Establishing the geographical orientation of the photograph, he tried to calculate from the shadows on the balls which image was taken first, but this proved impossible. He zoomed ever closer into the image, eventually finding a solution, of a sort, in the movement of little stones in the vicinity of the balls.

'When the rocks are uphill,' Morris concluded, 'the cannonballs are off the road. Then, you look at the rocks after they have been dislodged – rocks that were kicked and then tumbled downhill – the cannonballs are on the road... It is the laws of gravity that allow us to order the photographs.'[7] Despite the conclusion of the essay, in which Morris confirms the assumption he set out to question, the obsessive account of his investigations leave no doubt that the order of the sequence of before-and-after images cannot be taken for granted.

THE VERTICAL GAZE

It was the demands of criminology that shifted the direction of before-and-after photographs from the horizontal to the vertical. In the first decade of the 20th century, Alphonse Bertillon, a French police officer who invented such modern forensic techniques as the mug shot, conceived of a special contraption that he called the *plongeur* (diver in French). The *plongeur* consisted of a horizontally-facing camera that photographed the mouth of a periscope-like-structure, which directed the camera's gaze up to the top of a high tripod and then down again, affording a bird's-eye view of the crime scene. Bertillon thought that this vertical perspective avoided any of the preconceptions of subjectivity or positioning.[8]

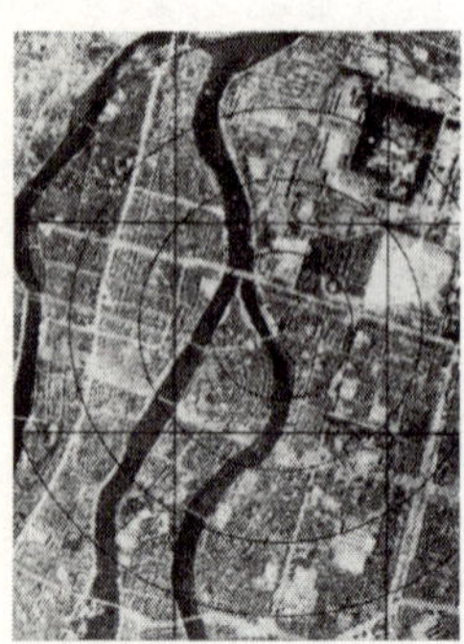

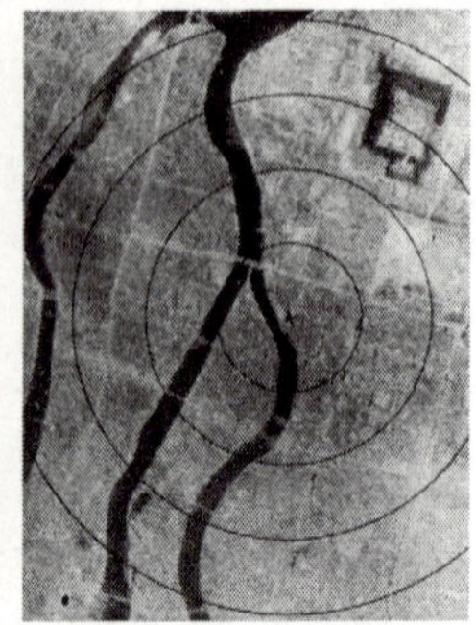

p. 58–59

Half a century later it was this perspective, taken from heights newly achievable by the aeroplane, that would document the annihilation of cities from the air by explosives, fire or nuclear bombs. In 1972, with the launch of Landsat 1, the first of NASA's earth observation satellites, a scale of environmental destruction well beyond the urban could be observed, gradually turning the entire planet into a site of forensic investigation.

In her masterful book *Close Up at a Distance*, Laura Kurgan discusses the ways in which satellite vision technologies have created a radical shift in our ability to 'use the spatial realm as a political, human rights and military reference point'.[9] Although satellite photographs are generally presented and seen as apolitical or neutral 'views from nowhere', they are in fact highly political products of Cold War-era surveillance technologies and other state logics.

Satellites, orbiting above the altitude of state sovereignty but able to see deep into it, are now a technology closely associated with the protection of human rights. For it is precisely the extraterritorial dimension of outer space (whose threshold is defined as the lowest possible satellite orbit) that makes satellite surveillance attractive not only to spy agencies undertaking reconnaissance missions but also to the international organisations and human rights groups who try to hold states to account.

Andrew Herscher importantly suggested that the fact that these surveillance technologies are used equally by militaries and human rights organisations is not without its dangers.[10] The Kosovo War at the very end of the 20th century was the first war in which human rights violations – those of the Serbian side, to be precise – were the justification for military action and thus the target for satellite reconnaissance by the US and its NATO allies. In this historical conjunction, human rights concerns and military ones were entangled, paving the way for further military actions (or threats thereof) articulated on human rights grounds in other conflicts worldwide.[11] Satellite images – purporting to show damaged, destroyed or cleansed villages and towns – presented in before-and-after pairs have become a call to action.

But Kurgan successfully demonstrates the ways in which satellite photographs – like any photographs – are open to different interpretations that cannot be controlled or contained by the state, and in fact can also be turned against it. The aerial perspective does not resolve the inherent ambiguities built into these photographs. Her book warns against the temptation of easy interpretation, of attributing to these images the power of conclusive truth beyond the need for serious interpretation. Rather than retreat from using this technology, Kurgan's work seeks to demonstrate ways to intensify the study and interpretation of these images, and to offer more creative ways of politically mobilising them.

Indeed, although satellite images are most frequently used by state and corporate agencies, in recent decades the practice of satellite image interpretation has helped transform the human rights movement from an advocacy-based practice to an investigative one that seeks to hold states accountable. Moreover, thanks to the wide availability of satellite imagery, even private individuals can now monitor the actions of, say, the US military. For example, browsing Google Earth, the Italian aviation blogger David Cenciotti spotted six US F-15 fighter jets parked at a newly constructed section of the Djibouti International Airport in October 2011, confirming that the Pentagon was waging a secret war in Yemen and East Africa. In other words, forensics is now being crowd-sourced.

p. 60

Satellite images shift the attention of human rights analysis from figure to ground – from the human to the environment. So how can human rights violations be seen without the human body represented? At a resolution of 20 m per pixel, as Kurgan has explained, human rights violations begin to be recognisable as environmental transformation: one can see, for example, the traces of mass graves in agricultural fields, but buildings and neighbourhoods are captured as an undifferentiated mass.

At the resolution of 50 cm per pixel – which is how most satellite images are made available – details come into view. Individual buildings and building parts can be identified, opening the possibility of architectural analysis. This interpretation resembles an act of archaeology. But this is an archaeology of the present. It does not consist of an earthly, material excavation of a distant past. It is rather an architectural reconstruction based on an analysis of images and the ways these images are composed in pixels.

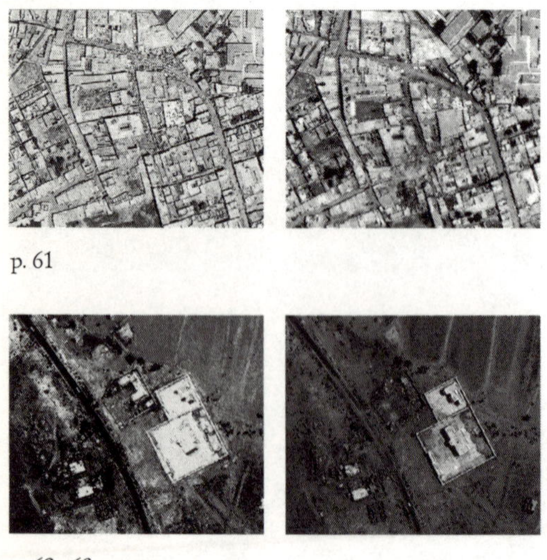

p. 61

p. 62–63

When crisis occurs, or is expected, commercial image satellites align their orbits to cover 'regions of interest' or 'areas at risk' in the hope of selling their images to organisations interested in the events below.[12] As such, they operate like photography agencies. The images they market are mainly interpreted by for-hire professional analysts who create before-and-after pairs and perform a skilled version of a 'spot the difference' game. Lars Bromley, a satellite image analyst with the UN, has explained that in order to create a photographic juxtaposition of before-and-after images, analysts must obtain each of the photographs through a different procurement process.[13] The 'before' photographs are usually retrieved from existing archives of satellite companies. These images might well be taken with no knowledge of the events that would befall the site photographed, although they are often taken in anticipation of them. An analyst most often searches for a 'before' image dated as close as possible to the time of the event. For the 'after' image, the analyst must either 'task' a satellite – which involves the expensive navigation of a satellite over a specific location – or chose the cheaper option of 'cherry-picking' an existing image, if a photograph dated close enough after the event exists in the satellite company's image bank. The image might already have been 'tasked' by another client (the buyer, whether tasking or cherry-picking, does not hold exclusive rights over the image).

In the analysis of the juxtaposition, the 'before' image is used as the baseline – the normal or normative state against which later events are interpreted as deviations. For this kind of analysis, the 'after' image needs to be as close in time to the 'before' as possible. The further apart in time the images are, the greater the margin of error, the more numerous the events that could be implicated in the new state, and the more speculation is necessary to fill the gap.

The fact that human rights groups rarely have the resources to task a satellite, and instead have to pick from existing images, poses a considerable limit on their work. Generally they can only afford to interpret satellite images of those places that are already being monitored by well-funded state institutions or corporations. It thus makes it harder for private organisations and NGOs to set their own agenda, and makes them dependent on the tangled interests of militaries, states and large international organisations.

p. 64

Sometimes, even when witnesses can point out the location of an aerial attack, no difference is detectable between the images taken before and after it. This is often because the impact or the entry hole is smaller than the size of a single pixel, which, as already mentioned, is 50 cm square at its sharpest.

In a case like this, one of the central principles of criminal forensics is inverted. Ordinarily, to interpret a crime the investigator (usually a state agency) should be able to see more, or in better resolution, than the criminal (whether an individual or an organisation). When the state agency itself becomes the alleged criminal, and independent organisations such as NGOs are the investigators, the problem becomes even more acute. Drone attacks are planned and executed by state agencies in much higher resolution than the one at which they can be recorded by satellites. Drones, we are told, can see the label on a piece of clothing worn by a person they are tracking, but independent organisations can only monitor the results of a strike at the resolution of 50 cm a pixel. The trace of the impact simply disappears within the solid colour of a single pixel. The difference between the high resolution of the attack versus the low resolution of detection creates a differential in knowledge that gives space for denial: the state can always marshal a higher-resolution image in order to prove their opponents wrong.[14]

VIOLENCE IN THE ANTHRO-POCENE

With the launch of Landsat 1 in 1972, politics became visibly etched on the surface of the planet like a long-exposure photograph. Landsat 8, launched in February 2013, is the latest satellite in this ongoing programme, which has systematised the ability to observe and monitor the surface of the earth in a resolution in which individual features may not be visible but the entanglement of man-made and natural environment are. Terrain data from Landsat shows the way in which human processes have continuously transformed the face of the planet. The repetitive coverage of continental earth surfaces has made gradual transformation visible in long sequences of images, which can be superimposed as well as juxtaposed. The registration of visible, near-infrared, short-wave and thermal regions of the spectrum captures much more information than can be perceived with the naked eye. The sensors on Landsat allow for the monitoring of changes in vegetation pattern (forests turning into fields, for example), heat irregularities (bush fires), air pollution and even the presence of archaeological structures under a thin layer of earth, which often affects the pattern of plant life over it generations into the future.

These images have made visible what ecologist Eugene Stoermer and atmospheric chemist Paul Crutzen have called the Anthropocene, the geological epoch that they claim has already superseded the Holocene. In the Anthropocene, human action has become a geological force shaping the material properties of the planet with a power equivalent to that of volcanoes, earthquakes and plate tectonics. The designation, still considered to be a hypothesis, challenges the distinction between human action and the environment, between man-made construction and natural site, and thus, again, between figure and ground. To think architecture in the Anthropocene is to accept that human habitation is not simply built *on* the ground but that it *produces* new grounds.[15]

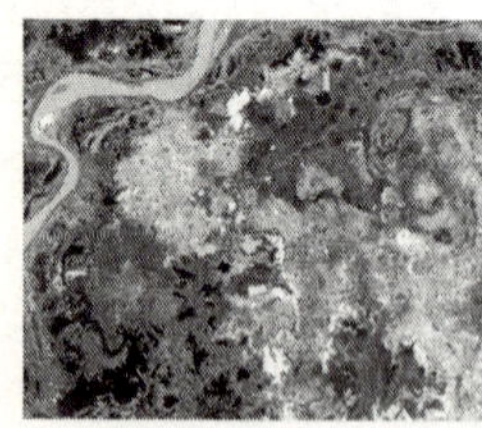

p. 65

The ecologists and geologists working on the Anthropocene hypothesis use the term as a warning about the effects that development, resource exploitation and global trade are having on climate change and about what they see as an approaching environmental Armageddon. The emphasis placed on this premonition of destruction can obscure the fact that much of the present level of human-material interaction is also the result of conflict. Conflicts in the Anthropocene might best be understood, not as battles taking place in the landscape, or even as wars fought for land, but rather as the process of making of new lands.

The history of Cambodia over the past 40 years, as captured in Landsat images, demonstrates the complexity of this entanglement of environmental transformations and conflict. In January 1973, less than five months after Landsat 1 reached orbit, the first detailed photographic survey of Cambodia was undertaken from outer space. That year also saw the culmination of an escalating campaign of 'secret' bombing unleashed by the Nixon administration. Almost 3 million tonnes of bombs were dropped on Cambodia between 1965 and 1973, more than on any other place before or since, and almost double the total dropped on Germany during World War II (1.6 million tonnes). Approximately two million refugees were forced from the countryside to cities; about a million of those crowded into Phnom Penh. The carpet-bombing ravaged villages, fields and forests, upturning the surface of the earth. British correspondent Jon Swain reported for *Sunday Times* in May of 1975 that the 'entire countryside has been churned up by American B-52 bomb craters, whole towns and villages razed'. The shifting of the topography affected the hydrological cycle, rerouted waterways and created swamps. The new bomb-made landscape demonstrated the central role war has in the Anthropocene.

However, the 1973 image became known not for what it showed but rather for providing the 'before' image – the supposedly neutral baseline – against which another crime would be registered: the atrocities sometimes referred to as the 'autogenocide' perpetrated by Pol Pot's Khmer Rouge regime on this very ravaged terrain, later known as the Killing Fields.

A satellite survey undertaken in 1985, six years after the Khmer Rouge regime was eliminated by communist Vietnamese forces, shows another massive transformation of the surface of the earth: a strange grid etched on the surface. This was achieved not by bombs but by the labour of an enslaved population that was moved out of the cities – including many refugees who had just arrived in them – for the purpose of excavating massive irrigation systems, canals, ditches and dikes. They were not built according to the lay of the land, but rather along the one-kilometre square gridlines that had been drawn for orientation on the Chinese military maps used by the Khmer Rouge. On the basis of this irrigation system, the regime could plan for the ruralisation of the state and the foundation of a sustainable agrarian utopia.[16] These canals cut straight lines through the ravaged ground of the already bombed-out Cambodian countryside. This massive project – alternately explained in Maoist terms as '

The Super Great Leap Forward', and in nationalist ones as the new Angkor (which had been built on a massive square canal system) – was the site of the Killing Fields.

The 1973 and 1985 satellite images thus represent the consequence of a compounded atrocity, inflicted first on Cambodia by the US Air Force and later by the Khmer Rouge, throughout the period that the Finnish Inquiry Commission of the time termed the 'Decade of Genocide'.[17] Of the two events, the US bombing is the less-represented episode of Cambodian history. Arguably that is partially because, although it was registered on the 1973 Landsat photograph, there was no 'before' image for it to be compared to.[18]

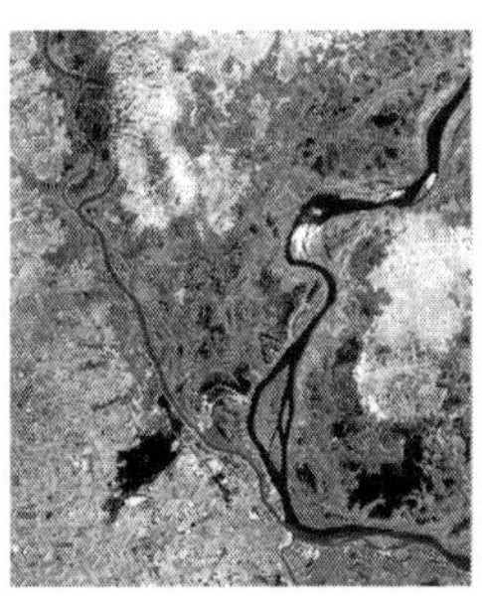

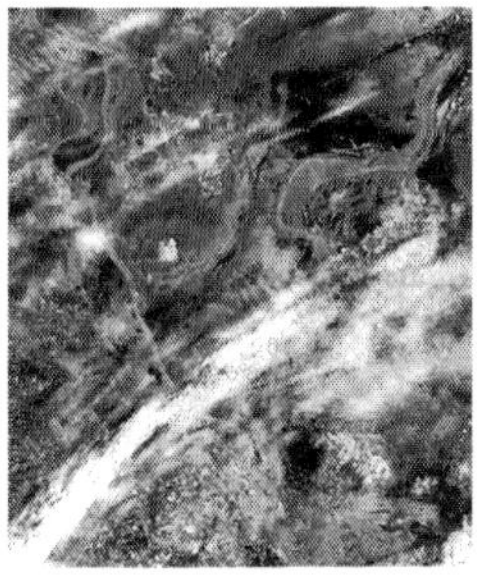

p. 66–67

The third major force of destruction that has been inflicted on Cambodia is climate change. Contemporary Landsat surveys of Cambodia show that the Khmer Rouge irrigation system is not only in good operational order but that it has, in fact, been expanded. This was done with the aid of the World Bank and other international institutions, and has accounted for increased land productivity and self-sufficiency in Cambodia. But even as extensive as the system has become, it couldn't handle the increased frequency and severity of the monsoon floods that have come with climate change. Cambodia is one of the countries contributing least to climate change but paying the highest price for it. In 2011, the worst flood in Cambodia's recorded history saw three-quarters of its land area inundated and about 80 per cent of the harvest destroyed. The case of Cambodia demands a shift in the frame of analysis, from a notion of human rights in relation to the acts of repressive regimes, towards a conception of rights that combines conflict studies with environmental issues. This concern has been named, by both militaries and human rights groups, as *environmental security.*

ALGORITHMIC VISION

The case of Darfur, Sudan, is another example that can help demonstrate the entanglement of conflict and environmental transformations. According to the UN, one of the reasons for the conflict in Darfur was a reduction in the extent of pastoral land, due to the desertification of the Sahel, itself a consequence of human-generated climate change. The tension that existed between groups divided along cultural, ethnic and religious lines was aggravated by the competition over a shrinking pool of land. But the transformation of the environment was not only the cause, it was also the result of conflict.

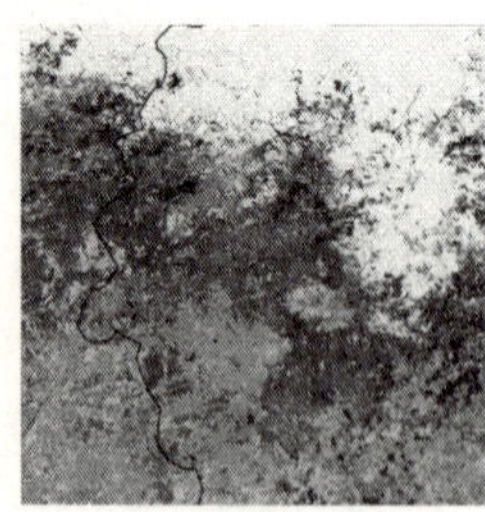
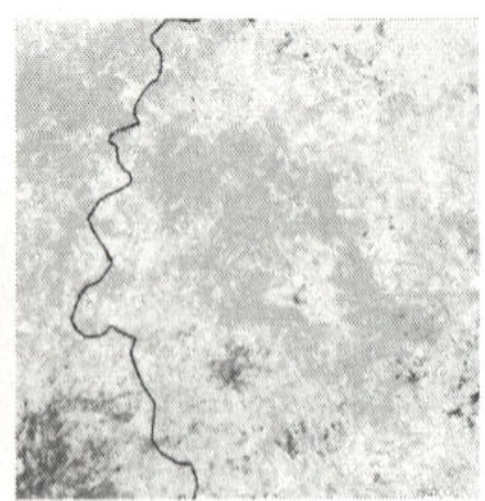

p. 68

In agrarian areas, such as those in parts of Darfur, where the conflict led to large-scale massacres and ethnic cleansing, cultivated fields have fallen fallow in the absence of their masters. Studying the transformation of the natural environment in Darfur, the Yale University Genocide Studies Program, which engages with the interpretation of satellite imagery to help expose and verify claims for genocide around the world, employed a satellite-borne technology called Vegetation Index analysis (NDVI). NDVI is a graphical indicator that is used to visualise the vigour of vegetation cover. When two or more satellite photographs are juxtaposed or superimposed, the NDVI data can demonstrate changes in the natural environment between the dates of capture. Each pixel on the image has a colour on a scale that indicates whether the area within the pixel lost or gained vegetation cover. Cultivated fields have a single plant species spread more or less evenly and therefore display a great degree of coherence in terms of heat emission. Several years after being abandoned, fields display a more random distribution of plant varieties, representing the robust return of 'natural' (uncultivated) vegetation, as can be seen in the images above.

The difference between the images illustrates a rebound in biomass, in vegetation coverage and in the vigour of the plants registered. Grasses and shrubs, more robust and durable than cultivated varieties, are now growing in formerly agrarian and livestock grazing ranges.[19] This, the Yale report claims, is most likely an indication of a decreased number of livestock and of farming activity – and thus of people – that followed 'the systematic government-sponsored violence and population displacement committed by Sudanese government and militia forces'.[20] So this return to wilderness – a process of nature repairing itself – is also interpreted as an area where humans were killed and displaced.

NDVI is a product of one of several hyper-spectral sensors that register wavelengths beyond the spectrum perceivable to the human eye. The digitisation of this data extends the capacity to monitor patterns of land use transformation as human rights violations across the surface of the Earth. Given the properties of an 'object' – a house, a vehicle, earthworks, a vegetation type – as visual or thermal information, an algorithm can identify and calculate its density and dispersion in satellite images. But even in this completely algorithmic environment, sequences of photographs are crucial. The 'before' image is significant because the baseline is calibrated to it. It is from this 'normative' state that the Δ (*delta*) marking the extent of transformation to the 'after' image is measured.

In this and similar analytical work, human rights violations are made visible by visualising and analysing some of the previously invisible domains of the electromagnetic spectrum. The exclusion of people from representation is thus complemented by their gradual exclusion from the increasingly automated process of viewing and also, as we have seen, from the algorithmic process of data interpretation.

In the advent of the human-rights movement in the 1970s, the function of testimony – mainly that of survivors and dissidents – was central. Testimony, reproduced in human rights reports and public statements, had not only an epistemic value but also a political and an ethical one. Human rights investigations could thus be said to be *about* the human and *by* the human. The shift in human-rights methodologies from human testimony to an emphasis on the analysis of material or digital evidence – which cosists largely of satellite imagery – has caused the field of human rights to give up something of what was distinctly 'human' about it. Human rights analysis seems paradoxically to have entered a post-human phase. Sensors and algorithms, rather than humans, are analysing the transformation of the environment as the condition that sustains human life.

We are a long way away from what scholars, thinking about the last decades of the 20th century, called 'the era of the human witness'[21] and well into the analysis of ground conditions mediated by algorithms. The departure of the human rights world from the traditional humanistic frame has gone hand-in-hand with the growing proximity between human rights organisations and the militaries of western states. This proximity, as mentioned above through the work of Laura Kurgan and Andrew Herscher, is expressed by a shared technology, optics, overlapping aims and a fluid exchange of personnel. While creatively using the toolbox of contemporary image analysis, we need to remember that the technologies of surveillance and destruction are the same as those used in forensics to monitor these violations. Both rely on reading before-and-after images, albeit in different directions and with different intentions. The air force targetier will study before-and-after images to evaluate the accuracy of a strike; the human rights worker will study the same pair to evaluate the civilian losses it has caused.

But even if the human rights analysts must look at the same images as the targetier, they can be tuned to other issues, establishing more extended and intricate political causalities and connections. They must see in these images not only the surface of the Earth but the surface of the image – that is the politics that is embodied in the technologies of viewing and representation. More importantly they should seek to understand the conditions – technological and political – that have generated the gap between the images.[22] This is because the gaps between the photographic or algorithmic representation in before-and-after images will forever keep the subject represented uncertain, discontinuous, lacunar, open to ever-new interpretations that will emerge every time we look at these images.

RUINS IN REVERSE

At its core, the fantasy of forensics is the reversibility of time. Before-and-after images can be equally read from right to left or from left to right, like the *Hotel Palenque*, which, in the hands of Robert Smithson, became a 'ruin in reverse' going through an endless cycle of simultaneous decay and renovation.[23]

p. 69

Another project evokes this oscillation even more clearly. The book *Bilddokument Dresden: 1933–1945*, which was published in 1946, attempted to represent the destruction of Dresden in sequences of before-and-after photographs taken by Kurt Schaarschuch. Schaarschuch photographed the city in 1933 in full splendour. A few weeks after the RAF bombing of the nights of 13 and 14 February 1945, he returned to the same sites, trying to find amongst the burnt rubble of his city the locations of the set of prints he had brought with him.

The caption he added to the last photograph in the book called for reconstruction. And indeed, after the partial reconstruction of some of the buildings, a number of photographers returned to the same sites captured by Schaarschuch, matching their viewfinders to his and creating yet more 'afters', which approximated the first 'befores' and which were reproduced in new city guides. This perception of the reversal of time is reminiscent of one of the most beautiful paragraphs in the literature of war, the fabulous anti-war utopia in Kurt Vonnegut's *Slaughterhouse V* achieved simply by inverting the description of the bombing of Dresden.

> The formation flew backwards over a German city that was in flames. The bombers opened their bomb bay doors, exerted a miraculous magnetism which shrunk the fires, gathered them into cylindrical steel containers, and lifted the containers into the bellies of the planes .... When the bombers got back to their base, the steel cylinders were taken from the racks and shipped back to the United States of America, where factories were operating night and day, dismantling the cylinders, separating the dangerous contents into minerals. Touchingly, it was mainly women who did this work. The minerals were

then shipped to specialists in remote areas. It was their business to put them into the ground, to hide them cleverly, so they would never hurt anybody ever again.[24]

p. 69

END NOTES

1 Conversation with Lars Bromley, 28 January 2013. See also the Land Remote Sensing Policy, 1992, available at http://geo.arc.nasa.gov/sge/landsat/15USCch82.html

2 William Fenton, *Why Google Earth pixelates Israel*, available at http://www.pcmag.com/article2/0,2817,2386907,00.asp.

3 Mary Warner Marien, *Photography – A cultural history* (London: Laurence King, 2006), p. 44–45.

4 'Marville worked in a methodical fashion; before the construction work began, he generally took two pictures – from two different vantage points – of each street scheduled to disappear. He then continued to photograph the site in each of the successive stages of its construction, thus outlining the layout of what was to come.' From Maria Morris Hambourg, in Chambord, Jacqueline, ed., Charles Marville: Photographs of Paris, 1852–1878 (New York: The French Institute/Alliance Francaise, 1981), p. 9.

5 Ibid, p. 10

6 Susan Sontag, *Regarding the Pain of Others* (New York: Farrar, Straus and Giroux, 2003), p. 53.

7 Errol Morris, *Believing is Seeing* (London: Penguin Press, 2011), p. 64.

8 Greg Siegel, 'The Similitude Of The Wound', *Cabinet Magazine*, Cabinet Magazine, (Special Issue on Forensics, Eyal Weizman ed.), issue 43, 2012.

9 Laura Kurgan, *Close up at a Distance: Mapping, Technology and Politics* (New York: Zone Books, 2013). The bulk of this essay was written before the publication of this book; we also consulted Kurgan's website, www.l00k.org, which contains much of the information later published in the book.

10 Andrew Herscher, 'Envisioning Exception, Satellite Imagery, Human Rights Advocacy, and Techno-Moral Witnessing', lecture at the Centre for Research Architecture, 4 March 2013. Herscher's lecture, although delivered too late to be referred to in this piece in more detail, has been instrumental in the edit. It was included in a series of seminars on satellite imagery titled 'Sensing Injustice' that Susan Schuppli has organised in the context of the Forensic

Architecture project. Other contributions to this series have been helpful in shaping this essay, including Lars Bromley's contribution, on 27 November 2012; that of John Palmesino and Ann-Sofi Rönnskog, on 29 January 2013; and of course, Laura Kurgan's Close up at a Distance, 19 April 2013. More information on the series is available at http://www.forensic-architecture.org/seminars/sensing-injustice/

11 '[T]he public could see ethnic cleansing in progress: high-resolution imagery of mass graves, refugees in the mountains, burning villages and organised deportations.' From Kurgan, *Close up at a Distance*, p. 117.

12 Andrew Herscher, 'Envisioning Exception'.

13 Conversation with Lars Bromley, 28 January 2013.

14 This information comes from an investigation on drone attacks in Pakistan undertaken by Forensic Architecture, a project directed by Eyal Weizman, for the UN Special Rapporteur for Human Rights. Participants in this investigation include Susan Schuppli (Project coordinator), Situ Studio (as collaborators), Chris Cobb-Smith, Francesco Sebregondi, Blake Fisher, Helene Kazan and Jacob Burns. More information can be found at http://www.forensic-architecture.org/investigations/drone-attacks/.

15 Dating the beginning of Anthropocene is controversial and contested. Curzon proposed the latter part of the eighteenth century, when the steam engine was invented. Others propose to go back a good few millennia, to the beginning of agriculture and settlement in the ancient period.

16 Robert Wellman Campbell, ed., 'Phnom Penh, Cambodia: 1973, 1985', *Earthshots: Satellite Images of Environmental Change*, U.S. Geological Survey, available at http://earthshots.usgs.gov. This article was released 1 January 1998.

17 Kimmo Kiljunen, ed., *Kampuchea: Decade of the Genocide: Report of a Finnish Inquiry Commission* (London: Zed Books, 1984). The Finnish Inquiry Commission estimated that about 600,000 people in a population of over seven million died during phase I, while two million people became refugees. For the second phase they give 75,000 to

150,000 as a 'realistic estimate' for outright execution, and the figure of roughly one million dead from killings, hunger, disease, and overwork. For more about the Finnish Commission, see Edward S. Herman and Noam Chomsky, *Manufacturing Consent: The Political Economy of the Mass Media* (London: Vintage Books: 1994) 260.

18 On the interpretation of these two images, a political debate emerged between the 'anti-imperialists' opposing the US bombing in Vietnam and Cambodia as a part of the US domination – most clearly exemplified by the position of Noam Chomsky – and the 'anti totalitarians', who saw the Khmer Rouge as a totalitarian menace that called for international intervention. In the late 1970s and early 1980s the exposure of Khmer Rouge's massacres in the name of a rural utopia, their attempt to rearrange the very fundamentals of space, and undo – once and for all – the division between cities and countryside which culminated in the evacuation of Phnom Penh, coincided with the publication of Aleksandr Solzhenitsyn's *The Gulag Archipelago*. Each in its own way exposed the horror of totalitarian-state communism and, to many in Europe, delivered a deadly blow to it. These positions accelerated the departure of a human-rights movement – anti-utopian and of limited aims – from the ranks of the radical left.

19 From the GIS & Remote Sensing Project, Darfur, available at http://www.yale.edu/gsp/gis-files/darfur/

20 Ibid.

21 The phrase "era of testimony" comes from Shoshana Felman, "In an Era of Testimony: Claude Lanzmann's Shoah," *Yale French Studies* 79 (1991): p. 39–81. Shoshana Felman and Dori Laub, *Testimony: Crises of Witnessing in Literature, Psychoanalysis, and History* (London: Routledge, 1992).

22 Ines Weizman, ed., *Architecture and the Paradox of Dissidence* (London: Routledge, 2013).

23 Robert Smithson, *Hotel Palenque*. More information is available at http://www.robertsmithson.com/photoworks/hotel-palenque_300.htm.

24 Kurt Vonnegut, *Slaughterhouse-Five* (New York: Dial Press, 1999), p. 64.

ACKNOWLEDGEMENTS

This text takes its inspiration from a chapter on before-and-after images in Ines Weizman's doctoral work on the architectural transformation of former East German cities, later published in various articles, but was refracted and taken further trough Eyal Weizman's work on Forensic Architecture. We would like to thank Alma (before) and Hannah Amalia (after) for bearing with us.

OTHER TITLES IN THE SERIES

BELYAYEVO FOREVER
PRESERVING THE GENERIC
BY KUBA SNOPEK

LESS IS ENOUGH
ON ARCHITECTURE AND ASCETICISM
BY PIER VITTORIO AURELI

CAN JOKES BRING DOWN GOVERNMENTS?
MEMES, DESIGN AND POLITICS
BY METAHAVEN

THE DOT-COM CITY
SILICON VALLEY URBANISM
BY ALEXANDRA LANGE

SPLENDIDLY FANTASTIC
ARCHITECTURE AND POWER GAMES
IN CHINA
BY JULIA LOVELL

DARK MATTER AND TROJAN HORSES
A STRATEGIC DESIGN VOCABULARY
BY DAN HILL

MAKE IT REAL
ARCHITECTURE AS ENACTMENT
BY SAM JACOB

THE ACTION IS THE FORM
VICTOR HUGO'S TED TALK
BY KELLER EASTERLING

ACROSS THE PLAZA
THE PUBLIC VOIDS OF THE
POST-SOVIET CITY
BY OWEN HATHERLEY

EDGE CITY
DRIVING THE PERIPHERY OF SÃO PAULO
BY JUSTIN MCGUIRK

BEFORE AND AFTER
DOCUMENTING THE ARCHITECTURE
OF DISASTER
BY EYAL AND INES WEIZMAN

ISBN 978-0-9929146-9-1

Printed and bound by Printondemand-Worldwide
Published by Strelka Press

Strelka Institute for Media, Architecture & Design
www.strelkapress.com

First edition.

The typeface used within this book is called Lazurski, it was designed at the Soviet type design bureau, Polygraphmash, by Vladimir Yefimov in 1984. It is a homage to a 1960s font designed by Vadim Lazurski that was inspired by Italian typefaces of the early 16th century.

Dresden, view to the Frauenkirche before and after its destruction, 13–14 February 1945.

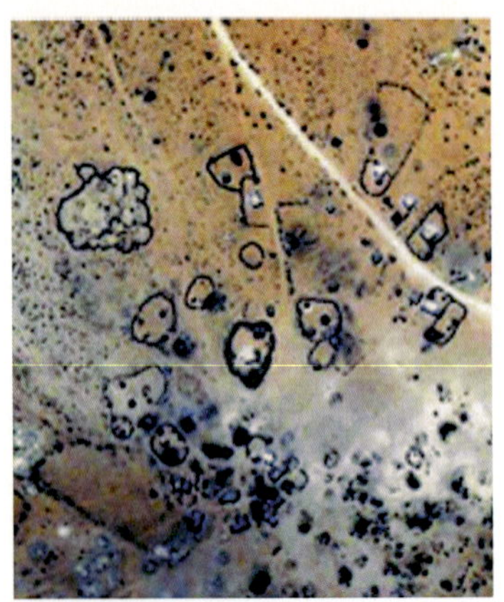
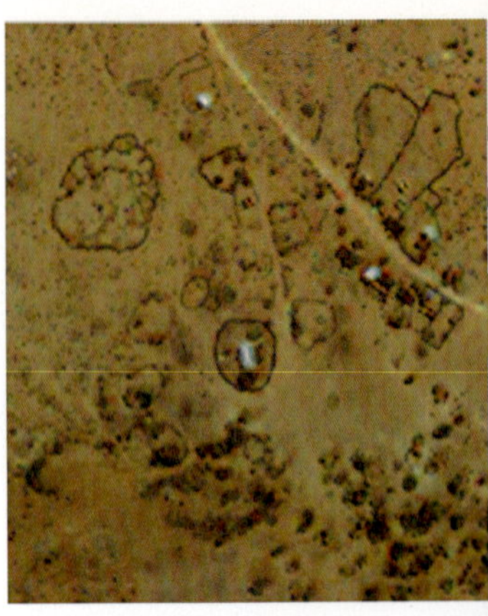
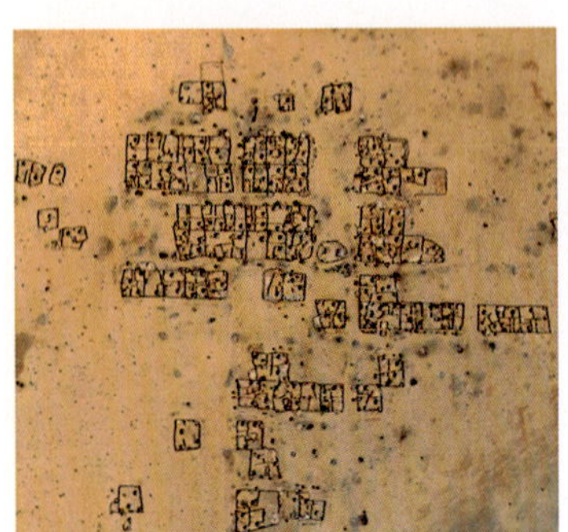
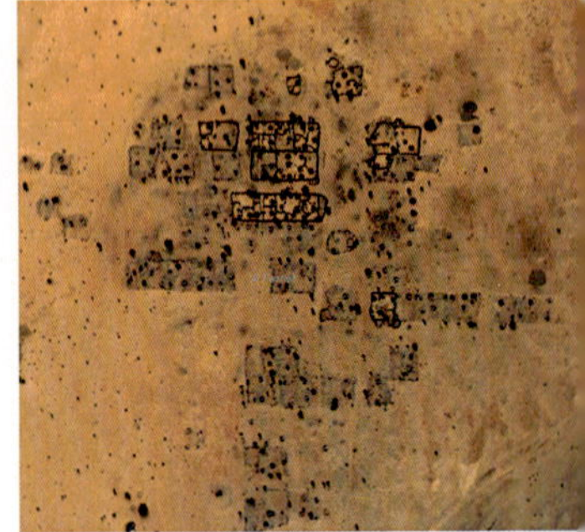

Top Senafe, Eritrea, 1999 and 2002.
Bottom Before and after destruction by the Ethiopian army.
North Darfur, Sudan, 2003 and 2006.

Before and after destruction by the Ethiopian army.
North Darfur, Sudan, 2003 and 2006.

ꝛoger Fenton, *The Valley of the Shadow of Death*, 1855.
Vith (left) and without (right) cannonballs.

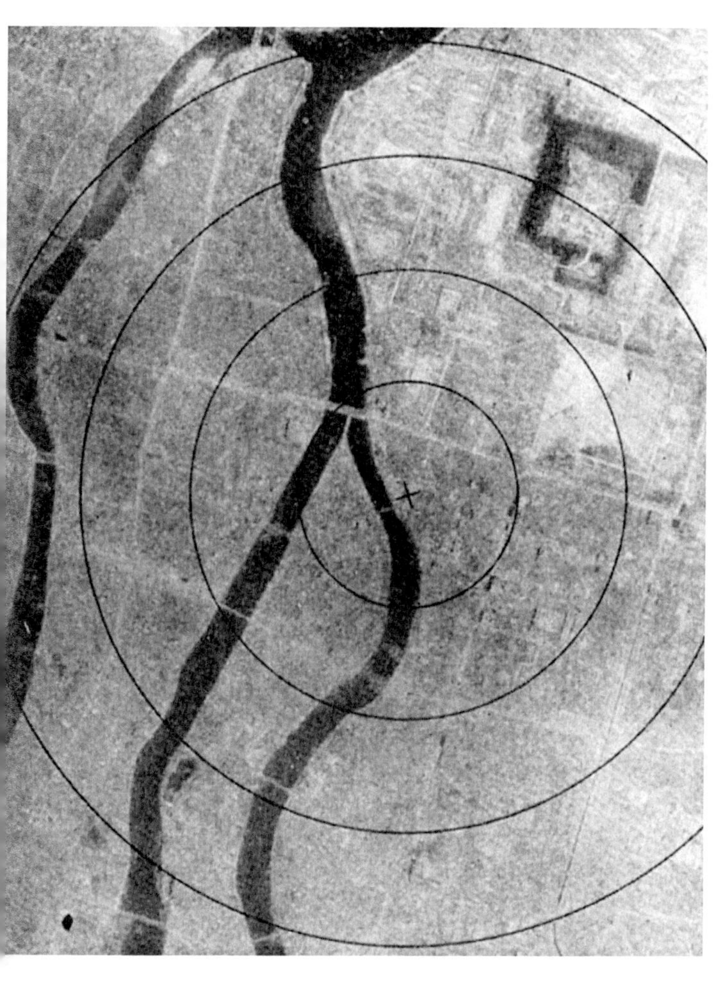

Hiroshima before and after bombing on 6 August, 1945.
The area around ground zero is marked with circles at 300 m intervals.

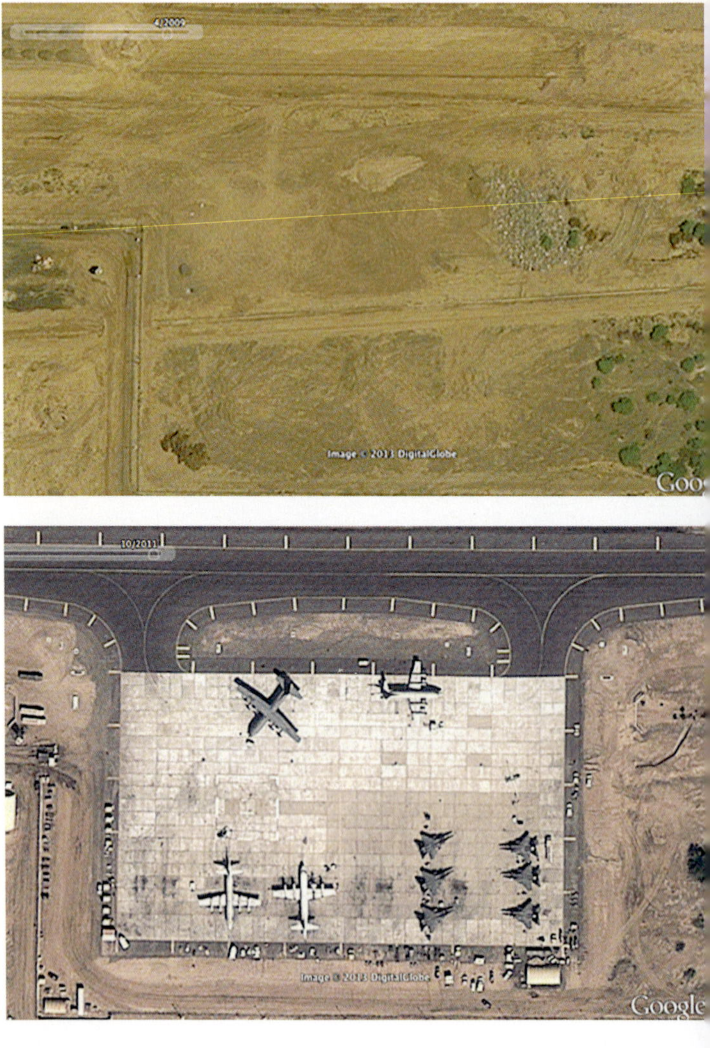

The international airport of Djibouti, as seen through the Historical Imagery function of Goggle Earth, April 2009 and October 2011.

'orensic Architecture and Situ Studio destruction of a weapons bazaar, most ikely by the Pakistani military, Miran Shah, Waziristan, April 2011.

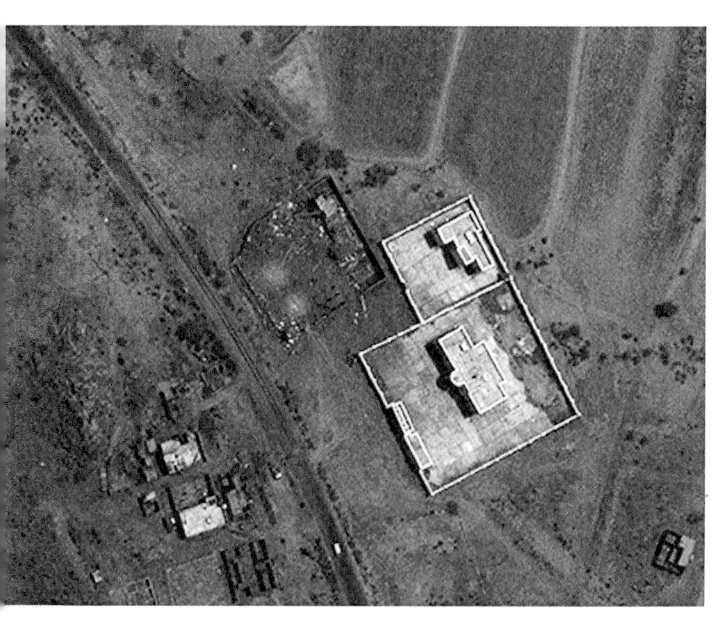

Forensic Architecture, the results of an American Strike in Yemen, 14 July 2011.

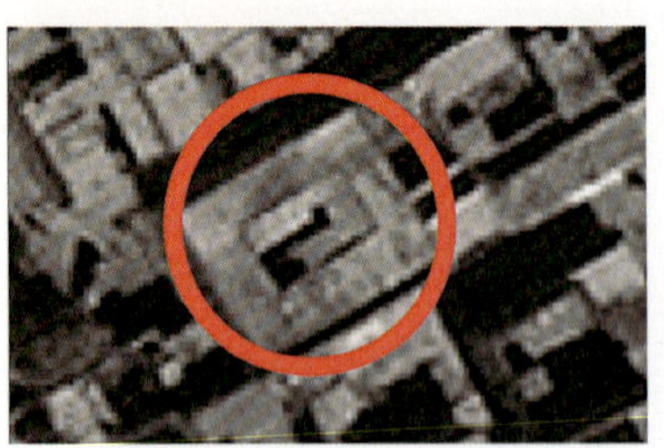

Forensic Architecture and Situ Studio, analysis of an alleged 29 April 2012 drone strike on a former girls' school in Miranshah, North Wasiristan, Pakistan. Note no difference is visible in this pair.

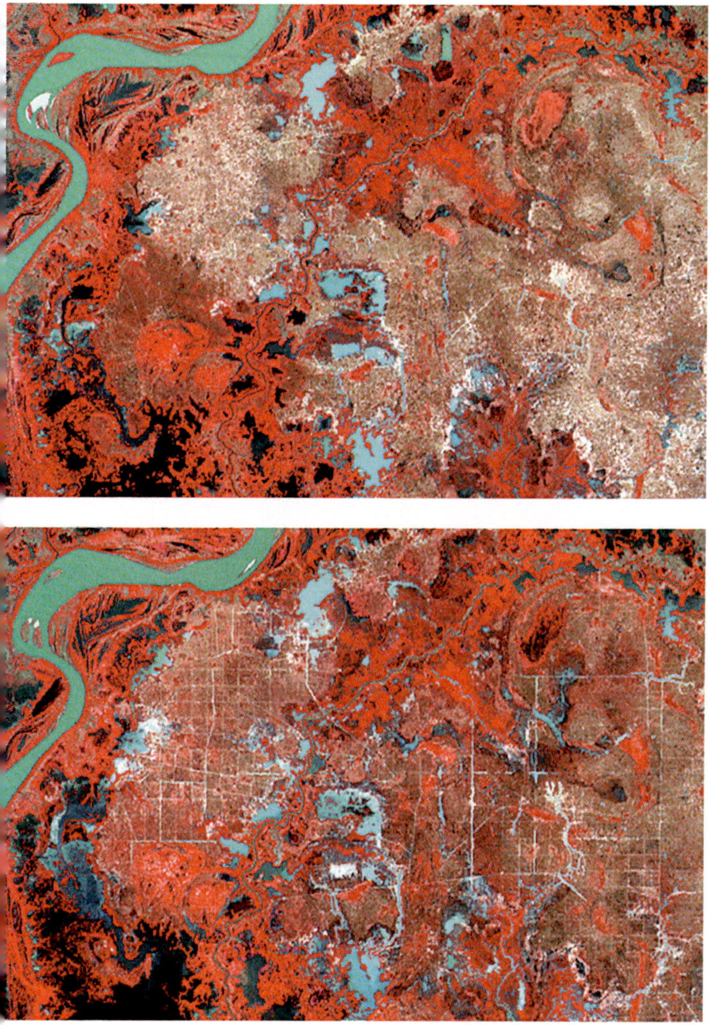

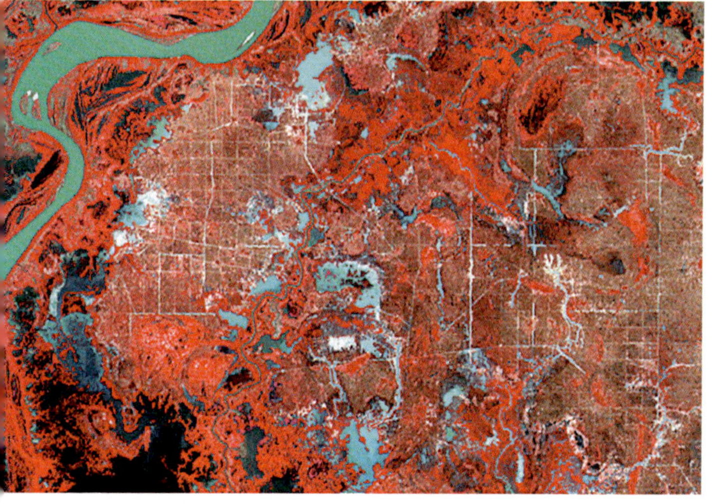

Cambodia, North East of Phnom Penh, Landsat, 1973 and 1985
Visible in the after image is a grid of canals.

Cambodia, the area near Phnom Penh, Landsat, 1995 and 2009 before and after massive flooding.

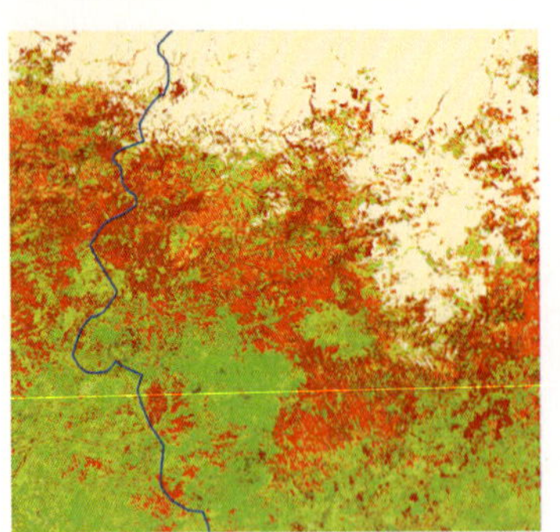

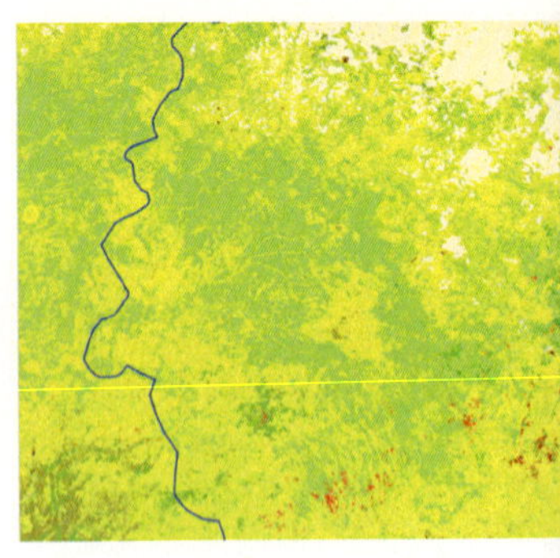

Darfur, Sudan, 2003 and 2007 Vegetation classification (NDVI) showing the increasing vigour predominantly of grasses and shrubs by 2007.

Top — Dresden, views over its destruction in 1945 and its reconstruction c. 1982.

Bottom — Dresden, view to the Frauenkirche immediately after and long after its destruction. Image on the left Kurt Schaarschuch. Image on the right, Stefanie Elsel, 2013.

IMAGE CREDITS

p. 53	Kurt Schaarschuch, *Bilddokument Dresden: 1933–1945* (Dresden, 1946).
p. 54 Top	AAAS, *Geospatial Technologies and Human Rights: Ethiopian Occupation of the Border Region of Eritrea*, 2002. ©2013 Quickbird – Digital Globe
p. 54 Bottom	American Association for the Advancement of Science (AAAS), *Damage to a settlement at the outskirts of Shangil Tobay/Shadad region* ©2013 Quickbird – Digital Globe
p. 55	Eugène Thibault, *The Barricade in rue Saint-Maur-Popincourt before the attack by General Lamoricière's troops*, Sunday 25 June 1848 ©RMN (Musée d'Orsay) / Hervé Lewandowski 2002.
p. 56–57	Digital images courtesy of the Getty's Open Content Program.
p. 58–59	Unknown Author; This image is a work of a U.S. military or Department of Defense employee, taken or made as part of that person's official duties. As a work of the U.S. federal government, the image is in the public domain.
p. 61	©2013 Forensic Architecture
p. 62–63	©2013 Forensic Architecture
p. 64	©2013 Forensic Architecture
p. 65	US Geological Survey, *Jan. 3, 1973, Landsat 1 (path/row 135/52) – Phnom Penh, Cambodia and Dec. 14, 1985, Landsat 5 (path/row 126/52) – Phnom Penh, Cambodia*, both ©USGS 2013.
p. 66–67	US Geological Survey, Feb. 25, 1995, Landsat 5 (path/row 126/52) – Phnom Penh, Cambodia and Jan. 14, 2009, Landsat 5 (path/row 126/52) – Phnom Penh, Cambodia, both ©USGS 2013.
p. 68	Russell Schimmer, "Tracking the Genocide in Darfur: Population Displacement as Recorded by Remote Sensing" in *Genocide Studies Working Paper No. 36*, Yale University 2008
p. 69 Top	Max Seydewitz, *Die unbesiegbare Stadt. Zerstörung und Neuaufbau von Dresden*, 1982.